24
Two-Part Inventions

Traumear

Paperback ISBN 978-0-244-33814-5

*

www.traumear.com

1

2

3

6

5

6

7

Goccoso

8

Slowly - with feeling

9

10

11

Adagio

12

Graceful

13

Moderato

14

Graceful

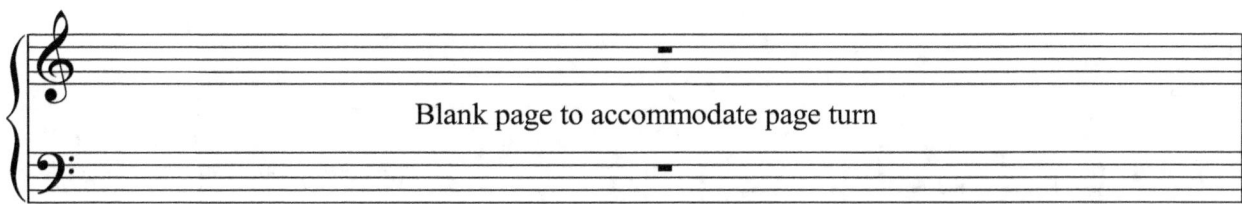

Blank page to accommodate page turn

15

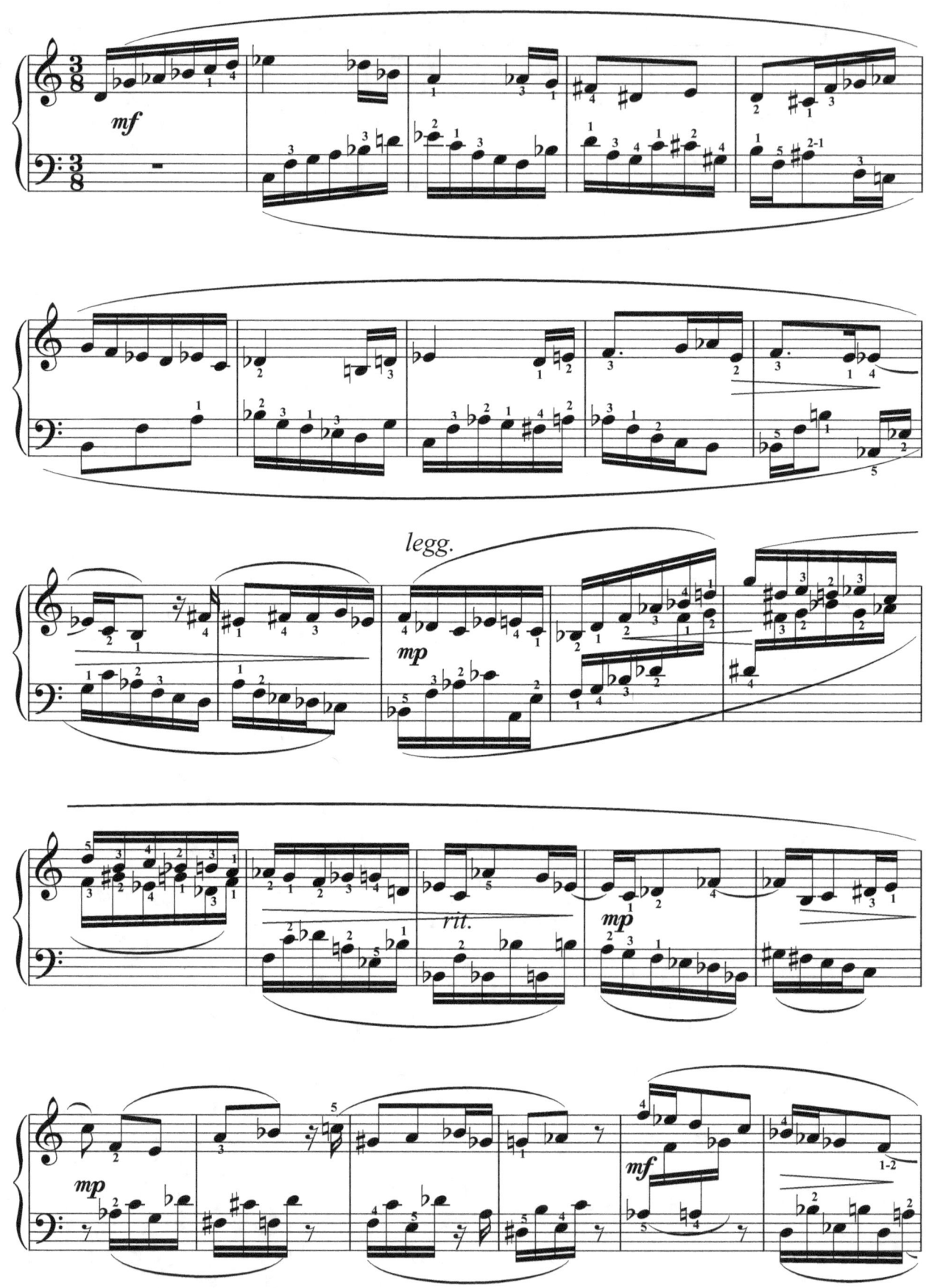

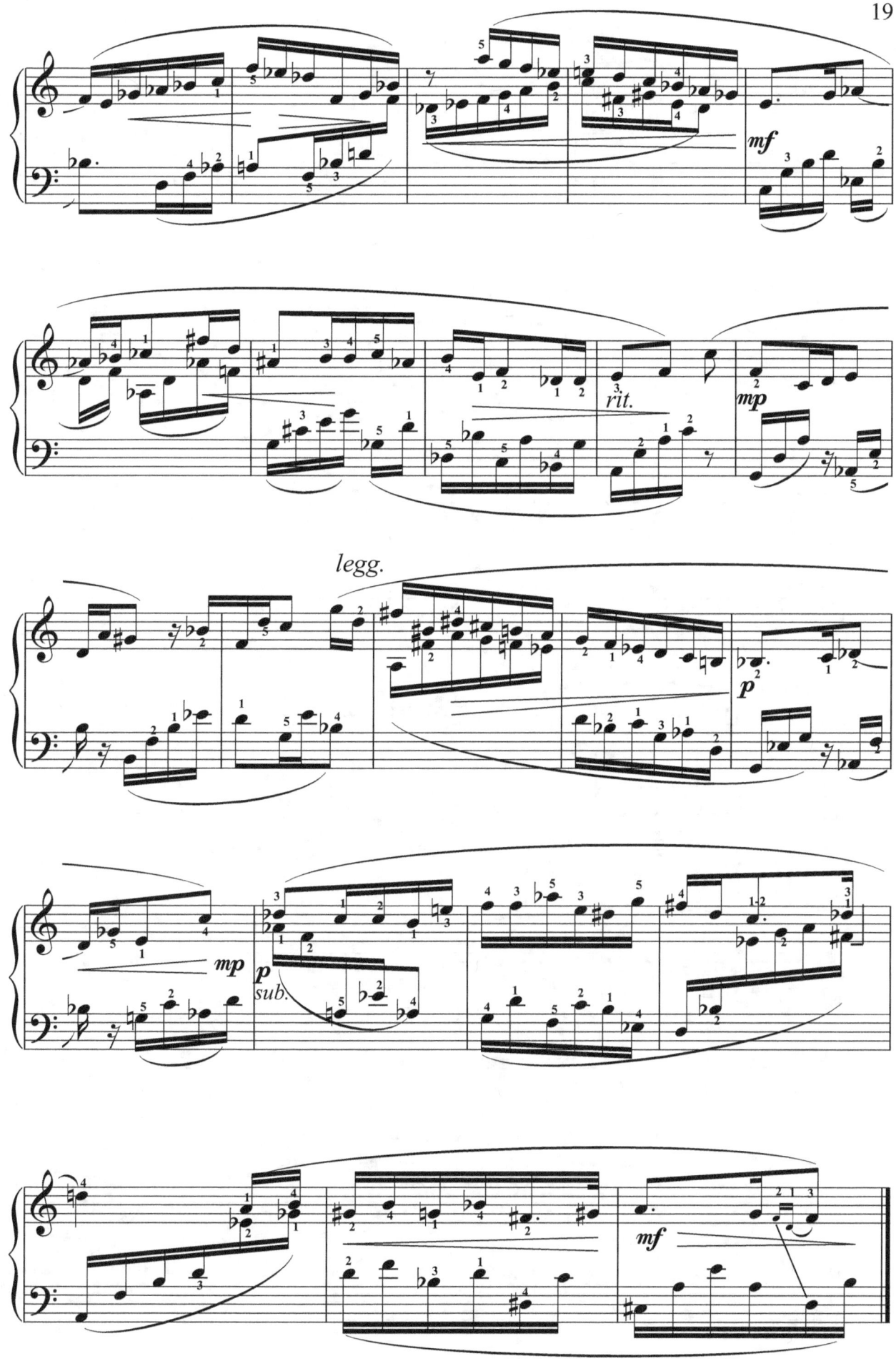

17

19

Not too quick

20

Largo

leggiero not too quick

22

Adagio

23

No. 24